FAITH INITIATED

Your Destiny is One Step Beyond Your Imagination

By Stephen Stone

© Copyright 2018 Stephen Stone

DEDICATION

This book has been directed from God and given into my life to share with others. I pray I have portrayed the concepts within the book in a simplistic and applicable manner as He told me. I dedicate this work to my wife, who has been the best thing for me in this life. She has been many things to me, but beyond everything, she's my soul mate and best friend. I dedicate my life unrestricted to God alone, who brought me through countless mountains to teach me Faith for the benefit of the multitudes.

www.stephenstone.org

ABOUT THE AUTHOR

Born in Walla Walla, Washington, I grew up in the Northwest in various cities throughout my childhood. I always felt there was a larger purpose to my life than living in a small town and growing up to work in a lumber store. At the age of 17, I graduated from a community college with an Associate in Arts degree and struggled with what was next. It seemed I was done with school, was working to make money, but still didn't know why I was doing any of it. Why did I need money? What was I changing in the world? What was I contributing? After 6 months at a lumber store I was offered a raise, declined it and joined the Army. I felt the Army would give my life a higher purpose and that I would be a contributing member of society, doing a great deed. Now, after 17 years in the Army, I realize it was God who directed my path back then, and still today. After having seen combat many times and been overseas for most of my career, I've experienced too many moments where even the men around me agreed that it was the very finger of God that acted on our behalf. My stories may pale in comparison to some, but they are the experiences that helped me begin to realize that victory came from a bended knee, not a proud chest. All these years I thought I had been so great and amazing, thinking I had carried such a huge responsibility and work load, all to find out it was God that brought me through it all.

God has blessed me with my soul mate, a warrior, my wife. I have been honored to raise our three children under my wife's supervision. My life is still just beginning, but I'm learning through new eyes to see all the things God has truly given me, and just how very valuable they are.

TABLE OF CONTENTS

1. What is Faith?............................9

2. Faith, do I have it?....................31

3. How can I initiate more
   Faith in my life?........................63

4. Faith Appendix........................105

www.stephenstone.org

INTRODUCTION

Whatever you believe you'll get out of this book, it's probably true. If you believe this is just another book on Faith that sits on the shelf, and won't add anything real to your life, then you're right. If you believe this book with its information will change your life, then you're right. You are already familiar with the steps it takes to initiate Faith in your life. You're also very good at accomplishing those steps most days, you just need some refinement as I did. This is a wake-up call to identify those steps that you're doing at least weekly, and re-initiate them for the right cause. The goal is to bring your Faith from being focused in the negativity of the world and re-adjust it to Faith that's not dependent upon sight or condition. To focus your Faith on a foundation of hope, love, and a future that looks brighter for you than anything you could imagine. You already have what it takes, it's simply time to initiate.

Let me assure you right now, this book is a very real approach to a spiritual facet chased by many educated people. It's not a book that requires a religious approach or mindset, but it is quite impossible to discuss a spiritual facet without also mentioning the ways the spiritual Father intended us to use it. By the end of this book, your Faith will unlock things for you that sat lonely in your imagination. It will give your Faith the rise it needs to stir you into action and result. As you read this book, keep a highlighter or pen near-by and use them to emphasize the seeds you need in this season. It may be one thing today, another next week, and something entirely different in six months. Lastly, included in this book are many highlighted quotes that I refer to as "Postable Moments", and they are there for you to post onto social media directly, or simply as a highlight to something I'd learned. If you post to Facebook, Instagram, Twitter, or another social media outlet, please type in the hashtag #FaithInitiated so we can comment and see the nuggets you're getting as well. I would love to read about revelations, life changes, testimonies of success, or even your own relatable stories this book may have stirred in you. Feel free to use the #FaithInitiated as you work through the book and make changes in your life to get to where you desire to be.

www.stephenstone.org

What is Faith?

Faith is not what you may think it is. I can tell you it certainly isn't what I thought it was when I started writing this book. Faith is most often referred to in combination with religion or a spiritual nature of some kind. I will tell you it's nearly impossible to speak of real Faith without mentioning spirituality. For example, if we take the concept of God, we can begin to study and see that the God of this world and creation couldn't possibly be as simple-minded as we are. Often, we say something to a friend and get the reply, "what is that supposed to mean?" If we can speak words having multiple meanings or hidden meanings, then certainly God can as well. *FAITH IS A SPIRITUAL LAW THAT IS SET IN PLACE, THAT MEANS THAT IT'S PROCESS AND RESULTS HOLD TRUE NO MATTER WHAT YOU USE IT FOR. #FaithInitiated*

Faith is multi-faceted, meaning all the definitions of Faith we cover in this book, hold true. For example, when you find your first girlfriend or boyfriend and friends or parents ask you what they're like, you don't simply say, "they're my boyfriend/girlfriend" and leave it at that. You describe all the experiences and actions that display your crush on them, the attributes they possess that stir you, what they say and do because it all has meaning to you. Yet, they are simply described as your boyfriend or girlfriend. In a similar way, the word "Faith" alone cannot summarize all the experiences and actions that go with it which brings its multifaceted definition.

We're going to explore the top three religions of 2018 by popularity and growth and briefly compare the ways they look at Faith as a principle. Also, I wanted to mention an interesting discussion I found including Atheism and its levels of Faith. For studies done in 2018, the top religions, ordered from #1 to #3, based on popularity are: Christianity (2.5 Billion people, 32% of world population), Islam (1.7 Billion, 23%), and Hinduism (1 Billion, 15%) [1].

The concept of God from the most popular religions is that God doesn't only love. He's righteous. He's a miracle-worker. He's jealous. He's merciful. He's worthy. He's holy, etc. However, most use a singular word to describe Him. It is said in the Bible in **Hebrews 11:6 "And it is impossible to please God without Faith…"** If God is so infinite and capable in

---

[1] http://www.thedailyrecords.com/2018-2019-2020-2021/world-famous-top-10-list/world/largest-religion-in-the-world-fastest-growing/20404/

every circumstance, why would Faith be necessary to please Him?

"The basis of any religion is Faith. Faith is not merely conviction of the truth of a given principle; it is essentially the acceptance of a principle as a basis for action. Without Faith, a man is like a car without a steering wheel, drifting aimlessly upon a sea of doubt and confusion." [1].

If you go online and Google search containing the words "atheist" and "Faith", you'll find some atheists believe Atheism contains Faith. There's one quote that stimulated my mind among many, "The church says the earth is flat; but I have seen its shadow on the moon, and I have more confidence even in a shadow than in the church." This comes from Robert Green Ingersoll's essay "Individuality" written in 1873, but he claims he was quoting Ferdinand Magellan, although there's no other proof

---

[1] http://www.islamweb.net/en/article/134445/the-islamic-concept-of-faith

that Magellan wrote this according to some scholars [1]. Julian Baggini, a British philosopher, wrote an article on Atheism and said a few interesting statements. "So, if Faith is some kind of belief not fully warranted by reason and evidence, then, yes, the non-religious have it too." He also stated earlier in the same article, "If "religious" is a slippery concept, "Faith" is even greasier. In some of its senses, we certainly do see plenty of Faith outside organized religion. If Faith is a kind of passionate conviction, for example, then look no further than the zealous breed of atheist who not only personally rejects religion, but also sees it as an offence to human rationality. Like the religious, their core belief becomes the center of their lives, their moral compass, their blueprint for a better world." This article gives a great deal of information and perspective of Atheism and shows that religion doesn't necessarily define us. Just

---

[1] https://timpanogos.wordpress.com/2015/02/21/misquote-of-the-moment-magellan-didnt-say-it-but-its-still-brilliant-shadow-on-the-moon/

because I am of a specific religion, I may not attain to all the standards you assume from the stereotype. By saying, "Faith can also provide the godless with a source of salvation that is based more on hope than experience."[1] Julian does address that there are various ways to define Faith. Depending on how you may view Faith one could easily say that even Atheists have Faith.

"Faith has a great significance in Hindu devotional theism. In Sanskrit, Faith is known as sraddha or viswas. The theistic schools of Hinduism are Faith based, in which devotion and Faith (bhakti and shraddah) are central to spiritual practice; Faith in God, Faith in the scriptures, Faith in the teacher, Faith in the path, Faith in dharma, Faith in the possibilities of liberation, Faith in the inviolable laws of God. These are a few explicit forms of Faith, which are emphasized in the scriptures of Hinduism as the

---

[1] https://www.theguardian.com/commentisfree/2016/may/24/atheists-faith-religion-uk

highest virtues."[1]

What you should be starting to see is that Faith is not simply one word with one definition. I've heard people say that Faith is desperation. Well, that's true. In desperation, we usually only have a single need or option and it must happen for the situation to be resolved. Our dependency is fixed, and our need is great. Therefore, trust is not an option at the time, because it must happen. Faith is dependency on God. Faith is need. Faith is trust. Faith is total belief. Faith is the miraculous creative power of God. Faith is a seed that grows. Faith is required. Faith is an absolute belief in Jesus. Faith is a belief in self. Faith is seeing towards the future with hope. Faith is proof I will have change in my life. And there are many more. *FAITH IS MULTIFACETED, AND THE REASON THAT MANY PEOPLE HAVE BEEN SEARCHING FOR YEARS TO FIND OUT WHAT THE SECRET TO FAITH REALLY IS AND TRY TO DEFINE WHAT IS AT ITS CORE, IS*

---

[1] http://www.hinduwebsite.com/faith.asp

BECAUSE THEY'RE STILL ON A ONE WORD, ONE DEFINITION, ONE PURPOSE MINDSET.

#FaithInitiated

When Faith became a subtle hint in my life, I was deployed with my unit in the Army to Iraq in 2003. We arrived into Kuwait in May and drove into Iraq in HUMVEEs piled together in the longest convoy I've ever seen. We saw kids begging for food, smoldering buildings recently on fire, broken and burned tanks by the sides of the road, kids throwing things at our vehicles or rolling tires in front of us to make us swerve. As we closed into Baghdad the smell of burned flesh became a very real problem to strike from our memories. That entire deployment I was tasked to be on convoys every single day. The shortest day we had was 10 hours of driving around Baghdad, Taji, Mosul, and different Forward Operating Bases (FOBs), and back to Bulldog FOB. I had been shot at, shot back, sped away from explosions, had people throw things at us from above on bridges, and had Iraqi obscenities yelled at me for almost an entire year. I had countless hours of being assigned poop burning detail because there was no port-o-pottie or cleaning system on the base and the fesces had to be disposed of somehow.

It was a tough situation and a high-stress environment full of very real danger. To add to the stress, I didn't know who I was in life or what I had Faith in. I didn't know my purpose, my strengths, my weaknesses, my gifts, etc. It became apparent over the next months that God had His hand on my life and was protecting me at every turn. I took one day off that year from convoys, and that was the day our convoy was hit by an Improvised Explosive Device (IED), and it would've hit my truck.

Another moment God's hand was evidently on my life, I was on a convoy of two vehicles and a mere six Soldiers, leaving in the middle of the night in Iraq.

We were commanded suddenly to stop in the middle of a highway exit/entrance system, that some call a clover leaf, where so many IED's had previously been planted. We were ordered to walk away from our vehicles and divide our small group of 6 in half. We had to walk up and down that highway exit with spotlights, surrounded by houses, cars zooming past us in the road, unfamiliar people watching, and encompassing darkness. We didn't even know what object we were looking for with spotlights because one of our senior members didn't want to admit they'd lost a part of their personal gear. When we were more than 150 yards away from the vehicles and other half of our convoy crew, we turned back, only to find a junior Soldier had been trying to divert traffic. Since they didn't understand what he was trying to do, the Iraqis simply stopped in the middle of the exit and our convoy was now surrounded by a multitude of Iraqi vehicles. This entire situation should have resulted in our convoy receiving enemy fire, confrontation, arguments, fights, or more. Yet, despite the huge language and culture divisions, the vehicles moved out of the way, we mounted up, and returned to our base unharmed. It may sound uneventful, but I assure you that in 2003 Baghdad was anything but uneventful, especially on a lonely convoy at night.

So many similar events happened, others who didn't believe in God, began to exclaim to me how some higher power had to be watching over me. *THAT WAS MY WAKE-UP CALL. WHEN OTHERS WILL GATHER AROUND AND EXPLAIN TO YOU JUST HOW PROTECTED AND BLESSED YOU ARE, TAKE A LISTEN. #FaithInitiated* They were seeing something beyond what I was calling coincidence or chance. With all of this, I still didn't listen or heed God's hint. Instead, I went home on emergency leave at the end of my deployment because my step-father had died, and my mother needed help.

My step-father's unfortunate passing, along with suddenly going home from a combat area, caused more stress, fatigue, and emotional confusion. I was in very serious despair and depression after being torn away from 300 days of convoys in Iraq every day. In less than 48 hours I'd gone from combat, to being home in the quiet mountains with no one around except my mother. Even my familiar home was broken. I would wake up in sweats and panics during random naps, and bolt upright looking for my weapon, as I adjusted to the time zone shift.

In Washington state many farmers invest in speaker systems with gun-shot sounds which they place surrounding their fields to scare birds and animals away from destroying their crops. On one occasion my mom and I stopped to get gas and when a cannon sound emitted from a huge PA speaker across the street I immediately took cover by jumping into the truck and yelling at my mom to get in. At that moment, who was going to help me?

Time to decide. Much like the conversation Neo and Morpheus had in the movie The Matrix, the red pill, or the blue pill. "You take the **blue pill**—the story ends, you wake up in your bed and believe whatever you want to believe. You take the **red pill**—you stay in Wonderland, and I show you how deep the rabbit hole goes. Remember: all I'm offering is the truth. Nothing more."

In similar fashion, I either choose life and blessing and a path that may have its struggles, but it holds hope, or I give up now and allow the circumstances around me to conquer me and only accept a reality of the things I see and can touch. If I take the second pill, it chooses curses and death for certain because no one could've pulled me out. I've felt separation from God, I've felt darkness, I've felt loneliness and despair, and I've been in the place where it feels like your path has already been chosen because of the circumstances you're in. It's the feeling that things are happening to you and you can't control anything, and when you try to control it you only make it worse. In the midst of that horrible circumstance, I chose life; I chose hope; I chose a bright future. I made a decision that I wasn't going to go through my life merely so others would enjoy their lives, but I was making a decision to enjoy my life because there was more for me than what I knew in the moment. I decided to set my Faith and confidence in something I couldn't see and something I didn't fully understand. I was willing to live life on the edge, willing to be called any name in the book, as long as it meant I felt fulfilled in my heart. *THIS WAS NOT THE PLACE MY LIFE ENDED, BUT RATHER I WAS BEGINNING TO LEARN HOW TO LIVE. I MADE A DECISION. THE SACRIFICE TO CHASE MY PASSION IN FAITH WAS MORE ACCEPTABLE*

THAN LIVING A LIFE UNFULFILLED. #FaithInitiated

What do you do differently to walk in Faith? Accept these things: help, risk, limitless possibility, happiness, joy, who you are inside, your pace in life is acceptable, things will be different, challenges will come, dare to dream, you have something in you that other people need, you are capable of this path.

I recently found myself staring up at the stars, as I often enjoy doing before bed at night, and I was speaking to God. The perspective-shifts my spirit gave me during this conversation was, why am I looking up at the stars to speak to my Father? I've felt it was appropriate to do so for years. An unending and unlimited universe, a vast space, a huge Earth, and billions of children, it seemed appropriate to put him somewhere high to look over everything. Then, as my soul gives my spirit the explanation of why I'm staring at the stars to speak to God, it hits me. Why didn't I look at the clouds, or the tree that's 10 feet from me, or the grass in front of me, or the dirt under my feet, or better yet the air brushing past my face and breathing into my lungs. God is closer than the air I breathe. He's a good Father, one that is always near and listening. It's me, not Him, that put Him so far away I would wonder if He could even hear me. He's not far off at all, and He's certainly close enough to hear and understand. He's so close it redefines the word intimate.

For example, in **John 17:22-23 it reads, "The glory that you have given me I have given to them, that they may be one even as we are one, I in them and you in me, that they may become perfectly one, so that the world may know that you sent me and loved them even as you loved me."** If His word can divide the spirit and soul, as the Bible tells us in **Hebrews 4:12 "For the word of God is alive and powerful. It is sharper than the sharpest two-edged sword, cutting between soul**

and spirit, between joint and marrow," then God's presence is even more powerful and intimate. After all, we can't even define and figure out where the soul ends and the spirit begins. If the soul is my personality, my thoughts, and preferences, then when I get a revelation how can I tell if it's just more knowledge or an actual spiritual revelation? And if it's a spiritual revelation I've received, how do I know I have received it from the spirit instead of receiving a new perspective by acquired knowledge or bright ideas? Yet, God is able not only to plainly see us as spirit, soul, and body, but also to touch each one individually without harming the other and making His presence feel almost simple and natural. What's interesting is when I feel God telling me to do something, I've found the more I follow His instruction, the bigger the adventure or mission ends up being. The bigger it gets, the more I trust Him, because I can see plain as day that it isn't me, but Him.

I believe this developing trust walking with God is explained in **Romans 1:17 (NLT) "This Good News tells us how God makes us right in His sight. This is accomplished from start to finish by Faith. As the scriptures say, "It is through Faith that a righteous person has life."** This trust and Faith in God throughout our daily life is how we learn our walk and live our life in fulfillment. After all, "It is through Faith that a righteous person has life."

Hebrews 11:1-3 reads, "(MSG) [1-2] The fundamental fact of existence is that this trust in God, this Faith, is the firm foundation under everything that makes life worth living. It's our handle on what we can't see. The act of Faith is what distinguished our ancestors, set them above the crowd. [3] By Faith, we see the world called into existence by God's word, what we see created by what we don't see."

Here are a few more definitions that will help highlight and open some additional areas.

"Faith, in the sense in which I am here using the word, is the art of holding on to things your reason has once accepted, in spite of your changing moods."
C.S. Lewis, Mere Christianity

"Faith is an activity of trusting, committing, and relating to the world based on a set of assumptions of how one is related to others and the world."
James W. Fowler

"Faith is not the belief that God will do what you want. It is the belief that God will do what is right."
Max Lucado

"Faith is the forward movement in our life derived from a set belief in our future, so solidly convinced, that it's results not happening is no longer a reality."
Stephen Stone

There's a lot to think about through all the Faith definitions, but at this point you should see a pattern of similarities, and vast differences. What's interesting about Faith is they're all correct. Faith is so powerful it encompasses all these actions, concepts, experiences and much more. In the next section we will move forward into discovering what it looks like to have Faith in our lives or how to recognize if it's lacking. For more definitions of Faith from many more sources take a look in the Faith Appendix at the back of this book.

NOTES

_____

_____

_____

_____

_____

_____

_____

_____

Faith, do I have it?

Faith is a spiritual law. According to the Bible in **Romans 10:17,** Faith in God comes from listening to the Words of God, but Faith can come from hearing many different things. Faith could develop, decrease, be strengthened, or weakened from hearing opinions, negativity, disbelief, gossip, your issues with someone else that causes another to look at them under the scope of how they treated you, or perhaps even your own affirmations spoken aloud daily to shift a mindset or habit. The first way to identify your Faith level in what you're trying to achieve each day, is what you're listening to most. Is it negative music, co-workers' gossip, fighting kids, nagging or dissatisfied spouse, or more negativity? Control what you're listening to, because what goes into the brain will produce your belief that it will come to fruition. Fill your time with motivational audio that consistently tells you that you can achieve what you believe and you're capable of more. Stop others from dumping their gossip and issues onto you by inserting your newest excitement about chasing a new-found dream. Change your environment. Dr. Reid A. Folsom said it like this, "Faith is the most taught principle of the Gospel, but it's the least used."

    Do you ever feel like you're wasting your time following something? Pursuing something? Perhaps it's God, perhaps it's a business or a dream, or maybe even chasing a relationship. What's most likely happening is we're no longer looking at our path with the same Faith that caused us to start it. We are in a place of planting seed and not yet in the season of harvest, or maybe you feel like you're doing well, but others are telling you that you're wasting your time. Even still, others probably haven't said anything to you, but you perceive they think you're wasting your time and look silly or crazy, and you want to change yourself to escape embarrassment. In some seasons of my life, like many others, I've received a prophetic word over my life and jumped for joy and chased it avidly! Other seasons aren't the same. I receive a prophetic word from someone, but I instantly discredit it, or put a condition on it that I'll believe it when I see it. If sight is the opposite of Faith, then I should have seen in my response that I had no Faith for it happening, but rather I had Faith in the opposite. BECAUSE OF MY VIEWPOINT BEING DRIVEN BY MY EMOTIONS OR SURROUNDINGS, I'VE ASSIGNED MY EYES TO LOOK FOR EVIDENCE OF SOMETHING NEW NOT HAPPENING. I'VE COMMITTED MY ACTIONS TO ENSURING I DON'T

ACT TOWARDS IT. I'M FIGHTING MY OWN BLESSING AND MY FAITH HAS A FIRM STANCE AGAINST IT. #FaithInitiated If this sounds like a few moments in your life with something you desire more of and it hasn't happened yet, I urge you to consider what you're watching for and what you're doing to act towards it. Your Faith may be completely set in the opposite direction, and you're sabotaging yourself at every turn.

When do you stray or run away from God the most? When do you neglect God's hints, presence, His time, His ways or forget to study His Word most often in your life? For each person, it is a different moment. Take a moment now and ask yourself, is it when I'm busy with the big problems that I really need His help with? Is it when I feel like everything is fine, and I have no problems in life? Or is it when I struggle with the middle ground transition moments of life when I feel stress and struggle in a multitude of little things around me that just aren't working out? Rest assured, we all have a breaking point of struggle, pain, circumstance, stress, overwhelming moments, ignorance, or forgetfulness. We've all heard the saying that the first step in solving a problem is admitting that a problem exists. You need a starting point. Begin with identifying your largest distraction or toxic thought and crucify it!

WOULDN'T IT BE WONDERFUL IF TRUSTING AN INVISIBLE GOD TO HANDLE VISIBLE PROBLEMS WAS AS EASY AND NATURAL AS KNOWING THE DEALERSHIP WOULDN'T SELL YOUR CAR WHEN YOU DROPPED IT OFF FOR AN OIL CHANGE?
#FaithInitiated

This type of reality or mindset often contains a hidden assumption, and always carries with it a lack of explanation or understanding. The assumption: "of course the mechanic wouldn't sell my car". The hidden assumption: "he will do the best work he could on my car and only do what I asked him to". There was no explanation needed when you dropped off your car and put it into his care. You asked the mechanic for a service, you left your car, and left or went and sat down in total peace. You didn't go into the garage to check on his progress, you didn't sit over his shoulder or video tape while he was working on your car, and you didn't ask him to tell you the exact moment he was going to finish, before he'd even started the service you requested. You simply requested a service, he told you what it would cost and what your sacrifice would be. You agreed and maybe asked about how long it would take, then you paid your sacrifice and moved on in peace, simply waiting on him. You understood the service was worth the sacrifice and that he was better qualified than you to conduct your request. Sound familiar? It's how we're supposed to be with God, except Jesus already paid the ultimate sacrifice. We're supposed to trust Him to perform a service with us, to do it right the first time, to bring us peace while we wait, and to answer any questions we might have when we ask. He always does His part, it's us that have the trust issues, the timing issues, the questions, the requests with conditions, the lack of peace and rest, and so much more.

    Amid tough and stressful circumstances, are you a fight or flight type of person? The lens of how we see our situation, or its outcome is often molded by how we view our past and our future. When you think of your past, what are the first things highlighted? Positive experiences or negative ones? When you look to your future, do you allow yourself to dream of what you really want on the inside, or do you immediately try to make your future "realistic" and take away the dream?

GRATITUDE LOOKS ALWAYS IN THE PAST

AND REALIZES IT TOOK MORE THAN JUST YOU TO GET WHERE YOU ARE, EVEN WHEN THAT PLACE IS SIMPLY BEING ALIVE. HOPE LOOKS FORWARD TO THE FUTURE AND HAS A VISION OF GOOD THINGS WHERE THERE IS STILL NO EVIDENCE OF IT HAPPENING. #FaithInitiated. To trust God to handle every day of your life, begin by understanding that He's already been there the entire time. He's been watching out for you since before you were born, and He calls you by name. Then, after reflecting awhile on the many times it had to be more than just coincidence, look forward and realize that we're not in this grand creation of a universe without a purpose. Trust God that he has a path for you and a purpose that is beyond you.

IN THE SAME WAY A FATHER WON'T SIT DOWN AND EXPLAIN HOW A FERRARI WORKS TO HIS 2-YEAR-OLD, GOD WILL NOT SIT DOWN AND EXPLAIN HIS PLAN AND PURPOSE TO YOU.

BY THE TIME YOU'RE READY TO HANDLE YOUR PURPOSE, YOU'LL HAVE THE KNOWLEDGE NEEDED TO BE VICTORIOUS AT IT. #FaithInitiated

So why is it harder to spend time with God and remember Him when we need His help the most? What has to change inside ourselves to keep us from worshiping, praising, learning, and loving on Sunday at church into a Monday filled with no time to pray, no time for choir rehearsal, and no way to study His Word? What takes us from observing "church folk" from a distance and disqualifying a worship encounter, or giving God any kind of chance in our life, into a true encounter and relationship with a very real God that's closer than we'd ever thought? It takes a wake-up call. The type that refuses to go back to sleep, much like the Matrix movie where once you take that red pill, there's no going back.

Every person on this earth has a breaking point before God. If that weren't true then He wouldn't be able to say that every knee shall bow, and every tongue confess that Jesus is Lord. **Romans 14:11 - For the Scriptures say, "'As surely as I live,' says the LORD, every knee will bend to me, and every tongue will confess and give praise to God."(NLT)** The reason all will break before God is sometimes misconstrued. The only thing in this world that completely conquers evil is love. I interject here to state that love is a requirement for hope and hope a requirement for positive Faith. If you want to look forward in negative Faith, then you need only highlight the limiting ways of this world and be creative in what disaster lies ahead. In negative Faith, only a solidified belief is required to match the depressing confession leaving expectant lips. *IN DAY TO DAY MOMENTS OF EVIL, DAY TO DAY DOSES OF LOVE CONQUER, BUT FOR AN ETERNITY OF EVIL ON THIS EARTH WHICH STRIVES DAILY TO HARDEN EVERY HEART, THE ONLY SUCCESSFUL*

BREAKING WEAPON WILL BE, AND IS, GOD'S LIMITLESS LOVE FOR US. #FaithInitiated. There will be no knee or tongue left that will be able to withstand the loving call of the Father, Abba.

Pastor Jimmy Davidson Jr., of Ark of Salvation Ministries, is a wise man I truly call brother. We began to greatly influence each other in 2010 in South Korea where God caused our paths to intersect. Ever find that person who you seem to click with so well that it feels like you've known each other for years? We spent countless hours drinking coffee and discussing life. His powerful testimonies of deliverance from drugs, alcohol, racing, accidents, and anger really drew me in. Because his passion is cars, we were speaking about guidance and the GPS systems we use to get around. We began to speak about the times there was silence from the GPS, my stress and worry was the highest, wondering if I was on the right track. In that moment of silence our driving simply continues on, despite our worries or doubt. When the GPS is giving me directions constantly or giving me reminders of an upcoming change, then I feel like I'm on track and there's no communication problems. There are moments where I wish I could get all the directions for the whole route, or simply know where I'm supposed to end up, but I only get that simple, "turn left in 800 feet". Now imagine setting your GPS location and before you can even leave the driveway, it gives you all the turn-by-turn directions of the entire route. Nobody wants that.

There are times in life when God is not easily heard. Often when God is not easily heard it's because we're not still enough or quiet enough for long enough to hear Him speaking. For example, ever have the music turned up loud on a road trip, and then the GPS gives some directions, but you didn't hear what it said? Other times it may be that God doesn't need to repeat Himself and has already given us instruction that we have yet to follow. Then despite our doubt or worry, we need to continue driving on in Faith. Other times we must realize that God will not give us the directions for our entire route, or even the destination address, because our focus needs to be on what is right in front of us. Pastor Jimmy and I came up with the God's Positioning System (GPS) theory and all the ways He guides us but we're just not satisfied with the timing or directions because we don't have the Faith needed. Silence is not absence, it is more often the only indication we receive that we're on the right path. Complete Faith should be displayed by our quiet trust and continuing action.

Regardless of the reason for the silence, the Faith that God is in control and still there seems to prove itself necessary. *IF I TRULY BELIEVE THAT GOD IS ON THE JOB AND IS GUIDING ME EVERY DAY, WHETHER IN SILENCE OR IN GIVING DIRECTIONS, THEN I WILL NOT BE LOOKING*

AROUND FOR DIRECTIONS FROM ANOTHER STRANGER OR SOURCE. #FaithInitiated. The other side is also true. If I don't believe god is still providing me with communication or directions, then I will start to seek out other sources of directions and information to communicate with me. The bible calls this the strangers voice. **John 10:4-6, "When he has brought out all who are his own, he goes on ahead of them, and his sheep follow him because they know his voice. But they will never follow a stranger; in fact, they will flee from him because they do not recognize his voice. Jesus spoke to them using this illustration, but they did not understand what He was telling them."**

This passage speaks about the stranger. If we look at the timeline there is no beginning and no end to when the strangers voice stops or begins. The presence of the stranger seems like a constant option for the sheep to follow. First, the shepherd brings out all who are his own, then he goes on ahead of them to lead them, and his sheep follow. His sheep don't follow because he brought them, they don't follow because they recognize his looks, they don't follow because they recognize the path or direction he is going, they follow him because they recognize his voice. That means that if we are moving, we are following a person because of the voice we hear. God oversees bringing us into His fold, into His arms and presence, He is also in charge of leading us down the right path, but we oversee recognizing His voice and following. If we take our part seriously then we must get to know the voice of God, the character of God, to know the things He would say and what would be in line with His morals and principles. I'm sure we've all had a friend, spouse, or sibling at some point in our lives. A special someone we joke and laugh with, finish their sentences, laugh about inside jokes between the two of us, and know what each other is going to say before they say it. If a stranger were to show up one day and begin even talking to you on the phone, claiming to be them, you would recognize differences even if they were saying the same things. That's how we need to be with Jesus. We need to see the world through His eyes, see people through His eyes, understand purpose and character through His heart, and feel His presence even in silence. That requires Faith. Faith says God is God no matter what else is going on. The focus in Faith is not on the circumstance, it is not on the present state of the world, it is not even on what is coming tomorrow. The focus of Faith is God. Sometimes people will tell me that I have the gift of Faith, but Faith is simple. Faith is not an over-powering feeling that causes people to fall out all around you. Faith is simple. Faith is the true focus and belief that God is God no matter what. All things are possible for God, even when things are impossible for man. Faith also agrees God's love for you will never be stopped. There may be questions even running through your mind right now, those are likely driven by doubt. The bottom line about questions related to God is we don't need to know. Total Faith doesn't have questions when it completely trusts something.

There may be circumstances and situations in your life where YOU'RE SEEING THAT YOU HAD FAITH BUT "NOTHING HAPPENED" AND YOU FEEL LIKE YOU DIDN'T DO IT RIGHT, BUT THAT'S THE STRANGER'S VOICE TRYING TO GET YOU TO QUIT. #FaithInitiated If you were to play a basketball game between the top two teams in the world and you told the second-place team (Satan) they had already lost and were going to lose in the end, they would almost certainly still play the game. If anything, it would make the second-place team play even harder to try to change that statement. The first-place team however, if they are told they will win no matter what, will be inherently lazy and over confident in the trust their star player, Jesus, will make all the shots needed, if they just show up on the court.

"Team Satan" will try to use any laziness or lack of motivation from "team Jesus'" and exploit their weakness to bring doubt to their team and conquer them in their minds first. Satan will still try to block shots, play defense, foul players, and double team you during the entire game. JUST BECAUSE YOU TAKE A SHOT AND MISS, THEN THE ENEMY STEALS THE BALL AND MAKES A SHOT, DOESN'T MEAN YOU'VE LOST THE GAME; RATHER IT MEANS YOU WERE WILLING TO PLAY. DON'T LET THE DECEIVER FLIP THE SCRIPT ON YOUR LIFE. #FaithInitiated

    Jesus loves when we believe Him and take a risk to show He's real. **Revelation 3:16 – "But since you are like lukewarm water, neither hot nor cold, I will spit you out of my mouth!"** Jesus tells us he'd rather we were hot or cold, but because we are lukewarm he spews us out of His mouth. Well what is lukewarm? You're not in the game, but you're not on the bench either. You're standing on the sideline debating the risk. You're focused on self. You don't believe you'll win, and you don't believe in the star player either. If any of those weren't true, you'd be on the court already, hot, and sweaty and on fire for God in every situation.

This can be more easily seen in **Matthew 14:22-33.** Peter is recorded as climbing out of the boat during a storm with high winds and waves when Jesus called him. Decision time, Peter decides to step out in Faith. This makes Peter a risk-taker in a huge way and the only possible way to explain the event is that Peter had such great Faith to get out of the boat. But what about the 11 other disciples still sitting in the boat? They were obedient to Jesus by getting in the boat to cross to the other side, but they weren't courageous or confident enough in Him to get out of the boat onto the water. To be known as someone who walked on the water with Jesus, it takes a courageous level of Faith and Holy Spirit led confidence in who Jesus is.

Faith is defined in moments or opportunities, but it's our lifestyle that is comprised of those moments and opportunities. People will never know that you're the person of God to go to for prayer until you start praying for people everywhere you go. <u>YOU DON'T HAVE TO ONLY BUILD UP YOUR FAITH FOR A HEALING, BUT YOU MUST ALSO BUILD UP YOUR FAITH FOR A PRAYER. YOUR FAITH MUST BE INTACT ALWAYS, BECAUSE OUT OF THAT LIFESTYLE FLOWS THE HEAVENS THAT IMPACT EARTH. #FaithInitiated</u> When people talk about miracle level Faith it's so often painted as a huge moment or a big deal. But what about simply praying for someone on a street corner who is down and out?

We have to be set in a lifestyle of Faith that will keep us courageous and prepared for both. That means plugging directly in to the Holy Spirit every day. We get to know the voice of God when we dare to believe simply that He is who He says He is, and we are who He says we are. Jesus could also be looking at our investment or commitment as well. An old fable explains that a father and son sit at a breakfast table and the son asks the father about the difference between commitment and contribution as he writes an essay for school. The father tells his son to look at his plate and tell him what he sees. The son sees ham and eggs. The father further explains the chicken made a contribution, but the pig made a commitment.

We must be ALL IN for Jesus. Our investment in the Kingdom must be the same each day, our persistence ruling our every thought and movement. We cannot play on an all-star team in victory when we only attend to watch practice once or twice a week.

That's not enough to be proficient at anything, even your employer knows that. Your boss expects you to put in a time investment equal with your pay. If you don't deliver the time investment, they won't deliver the pay or allow you to be on the team any longer.

We need to receive the constant revelation that we are a son or daughter of the creator of everything we see. We are heirs to the throne of God with Jesus. The life we live has been designed by God Himself, and no amount of failure on our part can ever hinder God's plan of success for our lives. You must decide God isn't only big enough to handle the big problems, issues, and events in your life but also the small ones that happen day to day. The small irritations that "I should be able to handle" are opportunities to help us realize He loves us. He will take those small things and display that even alone we are worth all the sacrificing He has done and all the patience He has given. Once we've made this decision and set our

Faith in it, we have what the Bible calls the beginning of knowledge. Faith says I don't need to know where we're going or where I end up, I don't need to know my purpose and I don't need the details, because He alone is God. See, we want the details because we want to brace ourselves and analyze everything, so we can prepare and react appropriately to the situation. That involves doubt in who God is. When we do that, we are doubting that God is capable of preparing us for something, and we're doubting that God is capable of taking us through a situation by Himself even if you're unprepared and incapable. That need to know attitude says, "I doubt you God because I am good at MY life and I need to have some foresight before You just have me do something."

THE DIFFERENCE IN A LIFESTYLE OF FAITH IS GOD DOESN'T NEED MY PERMISSION.

HE ALREADY HAS MY ATTENTION, AND I'VE ALREADY MADE THE DECISION THAT HE IS CAPABLE OF EVERYTHING BIG AND SMALL.

#FaithInitiated All you have to do with a person who has a lifestyle of Faith, is lead them down the path. You don't have to cater to them, you don't have to talk nicely to them, you don't have to say it twice, and you don't have to worry about them being led away by a stranger's voice. In a lifestyle of Faith, the focus is not on how big or small I categorize a miracle to be, because God is able. In a lifestyle of Faith, the focus is not on big or small words in my short or long prayer, because God is able. In a lifestyle of Faith, the focus is not on the people or circumstances around me or the event that other people might see, because God is able. I get through fiery trials easily because I'm too busy staring at God to notice the trial. If you don't give it your time and energy, it can't build. Faith is harnessed when a person has no reservations or restraints in their thought-life. All things are possible because they're plugged in to the unlimited source.

Recently, I prayed for finances to come into our hands from the North, South, East and West and for everything that was owed to us, "to be released to us now in the name of Jesus". The next day we received a check for almost $10,000.00. Some people would stop there and say, "Amen!" Why? It's only $10,000 and my God is bigger than that. The following day we received a check for around $130 and $85. The third day an e-mail of money owed to us from two different places came in that totaled over $100. Awesome right? So where does the strangers voice come in? Two weeks later a certain agency sent a letter stating I owed them almost $800. I didn't flinch or give it energy. I didn't help create more drama and accept the snowball of lies. I went straight to the source in an act of Faith because God can abolish the debt. I spoke to a few different people because the first two people said it wasn't possible to get rid of the debt. The third person said Yes, they were able to completely remove the debt. One week later my wife receives a letter from a certain company saying we owed them almost $4500. Same God, so we talked to a couple people because the first person said No but the second person said Yes. Here's the thing, some people would have just paid the debt because God blessed us with the money to be able to do it. Ok, and while I understand, I still ask where the Faith is in that situation. If I believe God can send me money to prepare me for a situation in the future, fine. That's not what happened though, when I prayed I demanded from every cardinal direction that I receive what was owed to me in my finances and I was blessed in abundance. Jesus came so that I may live life more abundantly. Jesus didn't bring me debt, He paid my debt! I recognized Satan's ploy to try to steal my blessing and abundance, called his bluff and saw it for the shadow it really was, and he had an empty hand because God is God and we win. Now, if I simply say that God blessed me with the money before the debt, so the debt wouldn't be a major problem, then I would have freely given away my blessing at only a shadow of death. In other words, nothing had happened yet. Satan's desire was for me to flinch and react to the imagination in my mind that exaggerates his every move. The problem for Him was, I wasn't looking at his moves. I was looking at God's moves. I didn't flinch because I wasn't focused on the shadow of this fake reality he tried to create to trick me and lie to me that would make me voluntarily give away my blessing. If God can prepare me for the debt by randomly blessing me with more money, then God is just as able to abolish the debt completely. Do you see how we limit God daily based on our logic instead of basing it on His capabilities? Stop limiting

God and trying to make His capabilities fit into your situation in the way you think it should fit in. Believe God is able and allow Him in to the situation since He is limitless. His thoughts are higher than our thoughts and His ways above our ways. Let Him be Himself and stop giving Him guidelines.

If you pray for a person to be healed, then walk away immediately how do you know they're healed? You don't really want to know because you truly believe it was contingent upon you and your feelings and don't believe God did anything. Imagine if you believed your emotions weren't in charge. It wouldn't matter what you felt or didn't feel. God's power and presence doesn't wait for your feelings and belief. God can overcome every failure of yours to get to someone else. You should be determined to hear the testimony of what just happened and be ready to pray again. There is a lifestyle of Faith that doesn't affect moments in our day, it affects our entire outlook and focus in life.

In a constant fight against this judgmental and harsh world, we must be careful not to inherit the "what have you done for me lately" mentality. That's a dangerous state, because it means others could dictate how you are living and what circumstances you will endure. It pursues a path that may create isolation from others, can require affirmation from others, requires permission from others, or requires help from others. Others can certainly affect our lives, but what holds true is they can only affect our lives as much as we allow. Some will come into our lives and boost us to new levels, increasing our love, hope, and Faith in humanity. Others may come into our lives with their own problems wanting to know what we can do for them and never give a second thought to pouring back into the lives they just withdrew from. The one thing we all need to maintain is the final decision of how much we allow others to influence our attitudes, thoughts, decisions, and circumstances in life. _WE ALL ONLY GET ONE LIFE, DON'T LET SOMEONE ELSE LIVE YOURS. #FaithInitiated_

So, for those that are saved and zealous, maybe even a little radical for God and His love, it's an easy choice to jump and follow God with all you have. Others haven't reached a breaking point of failure, followed by the immediate warm love of God, with His peace and acceptance amid their moment of failure. In the times when it doesn't feel like you're winning at life, don't worry, he happens to have perfect grace to cover you. It makes your 'F' an 'A+'. I've always told my kids, "some people will learn something when another person tells them, others have to experience it anyway". This has always been referencing someone doing something the hard or wrong way and experiencing the pain when it could have been avoided if they had just listened to the advice given to them. However, the same goes for

God's presence and love. The truth about a lifestyle of Faith, is you act in Faith already, I'll show you.

NOTES

How can I initiate more Faith in my life?

How can someone trust a God who is invisible and promises so much, yet is seen and heard so little? Well, who in your life do you trust right now? Take a moment and think about the busy day you had yesterday or today and what that friend would have or could have done to help you? Anything? Maybe a few tasks they could have done for you, maybe lifted your spirits, or brought you a coffee or a beer? But to get that, you'd have to initiate a conversation wouldn't you. You would have to reach out with a text or maybe a phone call. You'd have to ask for something and then wait for them to go get it or even see if they were available to help at all. That's called a step. It's a step that began in the realm and spirit of your hope. You hoped they could help, but there was no solid evidence they would be able to, until you reached out to ask, tell, or communicate. The step is known as Faith. Faith is demonstrating your belief in your hope, which looks forward into the future to accomplish something good or pleasurable for you. Faith has nothing to do with the amount of planning that has or hasn't taken place to get to point B, but rather enough courage and hope to leave point A. <u>YOU DON'T HAVE TO ALWAYS KNOW THE ENTIRE PLAN, BECAUSE IT WILL CHANGE ALONG THE WAY, YOU JUST NEED TO ACT IN FAITH ENOUGH TO WALK AWAY FROM WHERE YOU ARE NOW.</u> #FaithInitiated

Remember, always be careful when you place

Faith in people. The problem with Faith in people is that we're all flawed. We will all fail each other at some point. It doesn't matter how perfect or strong your intentions are because the result will not always be perfect and strong. Through no fault of our own, we will nearly always fall short of our promises and intentions. If you've chosen to put Faith in someone, don't base it on their performance, their ability, or their follow-thru, but rather their heart condition and intentions.

There could be several reasons for our numerous flaws, but there is one I see that shines above all others. It is to increase our dependency on God by seeing our flaws and failures up close on a regular basis. God is the only one that can make amazingly beautiful things out of mere dust and create spiritual laws that would hold a universe in place, while still ensuring the small, and temporary. Lilies of the field are fed with soil, rain, and clothed in wonderful colors. From everything it takes to survive and sustain life, to the visual pleasantries contained in the earth, God is ever-present. If only we were able to take our mind off our daily tasks at work, which seem to increase each day, and stop getting so stuck on things that seem to only get accomplished correctly when we do them. Just look around and smile at all the other creations of God, all your brothers and sisters on this earth. See the ones God clothed, fed, protected, healed from their cold, gave them a promotion, found them a spouse to admire, got them a job sitting next to you, and more. Realize you have a front row seat at Jesus' feet and observe His great and abundant daily works. When you can begin to adjust your perspective in this way, Faith will come naturally. TO BEGIN TO THINK THAT THIS IS YOUR WORLD AND EVERYONE ELSE IS JUST LIVING IN IT, WOULD NOT BE A FAR STRETCH.

#FaithInitiated These "pauses" in our busy day create

a moment when we're able to initiate a conversation with the One who has earned our trust since the beginning of the first clock and before. The very fingerprint of God is all over your life in more ways than you could calculate, and I could list here. The key to this, is keeping eyes looking to the future, where God is focused. Our negative enemy wants you distracted, depressed, disheartened, and discouraged regarding your current circumstances and your future, don't give him the satisfaction.

    My dad used to tell me a story all the time when I was just a kid. The story is about a man in pride who believes he has finally figured out the greatest miracle of all and doesn't need God anymore. This man works for years and finally figures out how to create life, so he calls on God by yelling out-loud, "Alright God, I finally figured out how to create life from dust! I don't need you anymore, I've done it!". God soon shows up in amusement and agrees to witness his miracle. God transports them to the desert of sand and dust where He created man and says, "ok, let's see it, I can't wait." So, the driven and prideful man steps back, bends down and picks up a hand full of dust. God quickly stops him and says, "Now wait a minute, let's be fair, use your own dust." I tend to remember this story and recall it whenever I feel I've "figured things out".

When we look forward in our future with hope in the promises of God then we can accurately count the cost of believing Him and the path of sacrifice it will require. After accurately counting the cost then we realize it'll all be worth it and make the decision to be all in with the life of Faith. We can look forward with joy and endure, even forget, any current pain we're in. For example, moments when I've been lost in worship and awe or praise, and time just seems to fly by, those are the moments when I'm so caught up in the presence of God that eternity is passing with each moment. In those moments, we can only bask in Him, His hope, His love, His ability to reveal what we're capable of, and in His glory. *WHEN YOU SEE, SENSE, FEEL OR EVEN NEED TO FEEL GOD'S TOUCH, PRESENCE, OR GLORY THEN THERE IS A STEP REQUIRED BY YOU. #FaithInitiated* You see, God never left, He's still there next to us, we just ignored Him because we got busy with unimportant but tangible things the enemy will use to devour us. God's still there but sometimes we need to take a step back and stop doing so much, other times we need to step aside and let Him do it because our way and timing won't work. Still, other times we need to leave embarrassment, pride, people, and all other distractors behind and just step forward into His solution with courage absent of excuses. That may mean a vacation to a quiet place for some, or a visit to a prayer closet for others. It may mean a career change or quitting a job.

My wife has never truly had to work since we've been married for us to make ends meet. We've been very blessed by that, even when the budget said otherwise. One of the things that attracted me to my wife was this sparkle she has in her eyes of life itself. She was working at a particular job for just over a year and hadn't been happy doing that job for months. She'd mentioned quitting, but every time she thought she was going to quit, she was overcome with guilt of letting me down and letting her employer down. When she finally made the decision in herself to let go of the guilt, and let go of the paycheck, and quit, she received the best affirmation anyone could've given her. The following month she made more money than if she had worked seven days a week at that job for 30 days straight. How is that possible? Faith. She and I made up our minds that even though the budget claimed we would take a hard hit, we weren't chasing a happy budget, we were chasing God, and He told us that He had everything handled if we would put His Kingdom first.

Any step towards god's control over your life, while trusting him to control it, is an act of Faith. There's something in this life that you desire to do that brings you fulfilment. Believing that God put that desire, fire, and passion within you to do it is also an act of Faith. <u>FAITH IS RISKY, AND REAL FAITH ISN'T SATISFIED BEING TALKED ABOUT FROM A COMFORTABLE LIFE. HOW'S YOUR FAITH WALK? #FaithInitiated</u>

There is a huge difference between a weekly revelation breaking point, and your life-changing breaking point. Our spiritual, life-changing breaking point usually comes well after we know everything about God and have perfected the actions and people-pleasing ways of being a polite, church-going Christian beyond suspicion. It's time to go before the God who has been with you already, through it all, and is waiting to love you. Sometimes the simplest processes are the hardest to walk out of, usually because we make them unimportant or disregard them because of their simplicity. Could it really be so simple? God saved us by words, belief in our heart, and repentance; remember easy and light is His style.

There are so many things to discuss in this process of what occurs and how to initiate Faith as a lifestyle, but the essential point is to get in touch with who your inner person is. Then begin to let your inner person's motivation to "get out" become your motivation to "move". Understand the way forward is to simply peel back your layers like an onion, and not try to force things to happen. What are you looking for? The fingerprint God left on you when He created you. Often the answer to the question, "who am I?" begins to show when you ask yourself, "what do I like to do?".

Motivation is different from Faith. Faith is an

action word and speaks of actual forward movement due to your conviction of something true. Motivation, however, is a general desire, need or want that generates the energy required for someone to behave in a particular way [1]. Motivation is also defined as the reasons why you are doing something, or the level of desire you have to do something. If you want to lose weight to get healthier, this is an example of motivation to improve your health. If you have a very strong desire to do something, this is an example of a time when you have strong motivation [2]. My summation is, motivation is based more on emotional excitement or feelings as a reason to begin or continue something but isn't the actual forward movement or the wake-up call event itself that could give you a perspective shift. <u>*YOU CAN BE MOTIVATED AND GO NOWHERE, BUT IF YOU HAVE TRUE FAITH, YOU WILL NOT HOLD STILL.*</u>

#FaithInitiated

There is a proper response to a wake-up call. Earlier I mentioned the wake-up call of a type that would make a person choose life or death without the option of returning. After my first Iraq deployment in 2003, a second followed a mere 7 months after getting back. The years went on in the Army and I became a Pilot flying Chinook Helicopters. My first deployment as a pilot would be in Bagram, Afghanistan in 2011. My team's mission was to conduct nightly deliberate operations that went after the bad guys in their back yards or favorite hang-outs. After a multitude of operations passing with shots being fired directly at my helicopter, but never hitting it, a few of my crew began to discuss this phenomenon of invincibility. One special night, as was my custom before every mission, I was out preflighting our aircraft and while I checked it, I was praying over it and our crews. One crew member named Chris had caught on to my tradition and began to follow me around the helicopter in silence each night. This night, a junior crew member had come up to the helicopter in the middle of my prayer and preflight inspection. He had his headphones in and was singing along to his favorite aggressive rap song, as loud as he could, because it was at the good spot ya know. Chris ran up to him and in one fell swoop grabbed him up, off the ground, and told him, "Be Quiet! Mr. Stone is PRAYING!" Immediately our junior crew member's eyes lit up and doubled in size. He corrected himself, took out his headphones, and silenced himself. I tried to tell Chris it wasn't a big deal, that they were fine, but Chris informed me they had discussed it and he wasn't going to let my prayers be interrupted! Chris grasped a wake-up call and made a permanent decision affecting that night, and nights to come. That's a proper response to a wake-up call.

Nearly every time Faith is mentioned in the Bible with the goal of describing or explaining it to someone, it is mentioned in an action or story from the past. Faith cannot simply be described by a set of words, but rather it's a mindset, heart-set, belief, principle, and perspective, all cultivated in actions that display something uncommon, outside the norms of most people. To do something beyond what you believe you're capable of doing, requires Faith. Everything that God does, is beyond you. Religion cannot sustain something God gave you. The traditions and routine of man will never give the fulfilment of the spirit. Faith will never fit nicely into any routine or tradition we try to fit it in. Faith waits for us, watching from beyond uncertainty, so that it may release the unlimited resources of heaven and display the impossible as probable. <u>FAITH THRIVES FAR BEYOND THE CONFINES OF EVEN OUR FARTHEST STRETCH OF IMAGINATION.</u>

#FaithInitiated

When we try to step in and create a routine, a science, or formula out of something that requires Faith, we insult Faith itself and will see an immediate decline in satisfaction, fulfilment, and results with power or success. You've taken something that was free and limitless and attempted to create a cage to fit it in. Faith is interlinked with freedom, there is no boundary or formula to calculate, only consistent action.

Faith is a daily decision that must be made. Psychologists say that the average person makes over 35,000 decisions every single day $_1$. That's 35,000 opportunities for God to interact in your life by way of your Faith every single day. **Proverbs 1:7 - Fear of the LORD is the foundation of true knowledge, but fools despise wisdom and discipline. (NLT) Proverbs 9:10 - Fear of the LORD is the foundation of wisdom. Knowledge of the**

Holy One results in good judgment. (NLT)

Above I mentioned **Proverbs 1:7, and 9:10** regarding the fear of the Lord being the beginning of knowledge and wisdom. Knowledge is the beginning of life, but it's only through ACTION that life is lived. Knowledge takes a back seat to action every time, regardless of the level of knowledge. Don't know too much. Sometimes when we believe we know a great deal about life or God we will say things that indicate we're foolish and know nothing.

To change ourselves, our environment, or others, we must act. Knowing something is right is not enough, it requires action to do what is right. In doing what is right, we see a righteous act. It's through action, or a lack of action, that people truly see who we are, because our passions and heart are the very source of our actions. **Luke 6:45 – "A good person produces good things from the treasury of a good heart, and an evil person produces evil things from**

the treasury of an evil heart. What you say flows from what is in your heart" (NLT).

Often, action comes from belief. When I have Faith that God will provide for me and my family, then peace and solidity will be manifest as an action. I may not be trying to display peace but, because of my Faith and belief, the action flows out of my fully convinced heart. Where my passions and heart dwell, action will overflow. The mouth is often a great indicator of where my true belief is currently located. Small indicators are, "this job is killing me", or "it'll work itself out, I'm not going to stress over it". *PAY ATTENTION TO WHAT COMES OUT OF YOUR MOUTH, AND WHAT ACTIONS FLOW OUT OF YOUR DAILY LIFE, AND IT WILL DISPLAY YOUR CURRENT SITUATION AND FAITH LEVEL.* #FaithInitiated

The estimation that an individual makes 35,000 decisions each day, is based on the average person on an average day. First, when was the last time you had an average day? Second, are you an average person? As your responsibilities increase, so do the number of your decisions. Add in kids? Add in a promotion at work? Married? Moving? Buying/selling something? In transition? These situations, and more, have an increased number of decisions to be made.

How can I possibly have Faith in every single one of these decisions? Lifestyle. If your concentration is to have Faith in every decision that comes across your plate then you will become overwhelmed, which slows down your decision making (realizing some are often time sensitive), and soon places the supernatural force of Faith into a formula, technique, or routine. When you do that, you insult what the very center of Faith is. **Hebrews 11:6** explains to us that it is impossible to please God without Faith…if you substitute the words routine, formula, or technique instead of the word Faith, it quickly displays just how ridiculous it would be for God, who is beyond time and limitation, to desire a routine, formula, or technique from your life at a minimum. Faith is a lifestyle of trusting, believing, and seeing. Faith shifts a perspective. Some say it's Faith that gives revelation, but revelation truly is simply a shift in perspective. God teaches us in moments of our lives where He gets to be the center of attention, often these are moments we would never choose for ourselves. God teaches us by giving us His eyes, or letting us see more into His heart, and that provides a drastic but subtle shift in perspective. God desires for us to see things in life through the eyes of life itself, through the eyes of love itself.

It's much easier to look at my entire day and ask myself, "how's my Faith?" or as some say, "how's my walk?". Misty Edwards gave a comparison at a Onething Conference in Kansas City in 2017. She gave the comparison of us in the spirit, compared to a new baby. She noted the similarities of not hearing things clearly from God, not seeing things clearly as He sees them yet, not being in obedience all the time, also not being able to have a perfect walk, but stumbling many times. Those sound like the traits of a new baby. Those traits include; hearing but not understanding; seeing but not deciphering correctly to negotiate things accurately; desiring to obey but unable to control everything we do; and lacking the strength, agility, and ability to walk as I see in my heart or mind. If I focus as a baby on my every single step or murmur from my mouth, I'll only get frustrated at my inabilities and focus more on my lack. If I focus on my lifestyle, I disregard my many misses and mistakes, I disregard lack completely, and I'm now focused on something bigger for my entire life, not just a single act or decision.

How can I tell if I'm walking or living by Faith? Look at **Hebrews 11** where the hall of Faith is. Many of the great men and women of Faith are listed here and are accounted for having Faith and righteousness. Notice, however, that it doesn't list their every decision that caused them to be counted as Faith -full or righteous, but rather it was the actions they produced in their lives. Your actions tell you if your Faith is lined up and working in full power and order. Words like "Faith" and "love" and "hope" are all actions. God desires for us to act, not sit by and be safe. **1 Corinthians 13:13 - Three things will last forever--faith, hope, and love--and the greatest of these is love (NLT)**. This tells us what will last forever, these things can never be taken from you. Under these three actions are where the investments of the Kingdom lie. Any act done with Faith, hope, or love will echo and last forever, and it will stand the fiery trials of judgment in Heaven at the end of this life. Each action committed within these three qualities grows that small spiritual baby into a beautiful, new, spiritual creature, which pleases God.

Faith is not limited by your imagination. Faith goes further than you can. Faith knows more than you do. Faith understands the solution to every situation. Faith is the creative power of God that exposes His solutions, His eyes, His heart, and His hands into your life. Faith knows no impossibilities but will alter any fact, boundary, or law to display the love of God. Faith says that God will do what's right and that He will do it at the right time.

After a few times of trusting in something or believing in something beyond what you see, you too will develop a reputation of Faith. The exciting thing about Faith is that it taps into a potential version of you, which you have no proof exists. It taps into a potential version of this world or your circumstances, that the world believes is not only unlikely, but impossible. God, the creator of all things, speaks many things about who we are, but it is very difficult for us to believe every single one of His declarations and walk it out daily. Imagine, this same God that created us and spoke so many excellent things over us, said it is impossible to please Him without Faith. It is impossible to please God, even as His creation, without believing fully in some supernatural version of you.

Faith is required, without debate or exception, to become something you desire. Faith creates your reality. This world has boundaries and laws, just like every one of God's creations, but we have been given the chance to alter and edit everything, as Artists.

In the Bible in the book of **Acts**, we get to read all about the critical times after Jesus dies on the cross and His team of disciples are left to carry the torch. Paul was not one of the disciples. Paul had a very real encounter with Jesus which changed his entire perspective in just a matter of minutes. Paul had such a powerful encounter that he wrote 2/3 of the New Testament material in the Bible today. That's the kind of Faith shift we're after here. Looking at the lifestyle of Paul in the book of Acts, there is a trend we need to see. Paul sets the pattern of Obedience in Faith first, followed by a consequence requiring a sacrifice, followed by a blessing that forwards the Kingdom of God in the Earth. Paul was given freedom in Christ and it stirred up his passion to share truth and the gospel. Looking at Paul with success principles in mind, he always performed his passion regardless of his surroundings, audience, or location. He allowed the Holy Spirit to be his guide regardless of how silly or crazy it seemed. He preached the same message in a multitude of different cities, before different Jewish counsels, before royalty, and before the poor. What can we learn from Paul about Faith? *BE WHO YOU ARE, WHERE YOU ARE, AND IT CREATES THE NEXT STEP #FaithInitiated* If Paul hadn't ruffled the feathers of a few audience members of the Jews, he never would have met Roman officers. He met the Roman Officers by getting arrested multiple times. He was beaten nearly to death multiple times. He only met royalty and court members because he was on trial. When he met them, he was true to the assignment he'd been given and stood in Faith. Paul changed their lives forever with his message. If Paul hadn't been thrown into prisons, he never would have experienced getting rescued by angels. He had Faith that everything was going to be all right and he had to stay true to himself always, regardless of the appearing result.

Also in **Acts, chapter 18**, Paul is alone preaching for a time and working to support himself making tents. He's staying with another couple that he just met, no doubt influencing their lives daily as they lived and worked together. However, things change when his friends Silas and Timothy show up. He now has a team and can quit working. He then devotes all his time to his passion of preaching the gospel. What is the point? <u>YOU CAN DO MORE WITH A TEAM, TRUST THEM AND LET THEM HELP #FaithInitiated</u>

Even Jesus established a team. He established a team to teach, mentor, change, impact, and multiply His cause and effect.

Almost every time Jesus mentions Faith or sees Faith in people, He displays the next level of Faith to solve the issue they bring. Read this interaction Jesus has with a Centurion guard in **Matthew 8: 5-13** from the Bible:

"**When Jesus returned to Capernaum, a Roman officer came and pleaded with him, "Lord, my young servant lies in bed, paralyzed and in terrible pain."**

Jesus said, "I will come and heal him."

But the officer said, "Lord, I am not worthy to have you come into my home. Just say the word from where you are, and my servant will be healed. I know this because I am under the authority of my superior officers, and I have

authority over my soldiers. I only need to say, 'Go,' and they go, or 'Come,' and they come. And if I say to my slaves, 'Do this,' they do it."

When Jesus heard this, he was amazed. Turning to those who were following him, he said, "I tell you the truth, I haven't seen faith like this in all Israel! And I tell you this, that many Gentiles will come from all over the world—from east and west—and sit down with Abraham, Isaac, and Jacob at the feast in the Kingdom of Heaven. But many Israelites—those for whom the Kingdom was prepared—will be thrown into outer darkness, where there will be weeping and gnashing of teeth."

Then Jesus said to the Roman officer, "Go back home. Because you believed, it has happened." And the young servant was healed that same hour."

With the Centurion, Jesus said he had great Faith because the centurion understood authority and didn't need Jesus to GO to his house. Instead of saying the words Jesus simply told him, **"Go back home. Because you believed, it has happened."**. Jesus never said, "servant be healed". Jesus takes us from where we are in Faith and displays the next level of Faith when He fixes the situation we asked for.

The Kingdom of God IS movement. When the presence of God comes into situations or places and is allowed to move, He changes things...He moves things. If the Kingdom were not moving then nothing would change, but it changes EVERYTHING it comes in to contact with. The Kingdom of God IS movement.

The presence of Faith is required for every miracle, or Kingdom adjustment on the Earth. Jesus adjusted others' Faith when they couldn't believe and performed miracles anyway. When the disciples couldn't do something Jesus always asked them why they had such a lack of Faith. He never accused the person asking for the miracle of being so lacking in Faith the miracle couldn't happen; rather He stepped in and through Grace was able to compensate the situation with His Faith and access the Kingdom to get it done.

So, let's talk focus and result for a moment. The Bible describes our focus as being attached to our heart in **Luke 12:34 – "Wherever your treasure is, there the desires of your heart will also be" (NLT)** or in the Message translation, **"It's obvious, isn't it? The place where your treasure is, is the place you will most want to be, and end up being."** God isn't speaking about a theory or emotions here, He's talking about design. He's straight up telling us exactly how our spirit, soul, and body are designed to work together. He gave us the keys to the Kingdom completely. He's explaining to us what can or will happen when we set our desire on something. When we set our heart on something, that same place contains its own specific treasure. James Allen wrote it like this: "Men do not attract that which they WANT, but that which they ARE. Their whims, fancies, and ambitions are thwarted at every step, but their inmost thoughts and desires are fed with their own food, be it foul or clean. The "divinity that shapes our ends" is in ourselves; it is our very self. Only himself manacles man: thought and action are the goalers of Fate—they imprison, being base; they are also the angels of Freedom—they liberate, being noble. Not what he wishes and prays for does a man get, but what he justly earns. His wishes and prayers are only gratified and answered when they harmonize with his thoughts and actions." – As A Man Thinketh, James Allen

In other words, every heart action holds its own reward, whether that's righteous and helpful, or unrighteous and deadly. If your heart desires prosperity, then your mind will follow your heart by creating ways to become prosperous and shift your perspective. Within that path, there is a certain treasure that will go with it. If your heart desires lust or addictions but your mouth speaks prosperity, then lust and addictions will continue and grow, holding their own treasure of torment. When you align your heart and your thoughts with your words and prayers, on the same accord, then whatever passion you chase will grow into reality.

Faith is not quantifiable. That means you don't get a percentage amount to measure your Faith level now, compared to later. We are given opportunities, situations, trials, and circumstances to experience our Faith level in life. In **Joshua 6**, there is an event that takes place where a people are told to march around the walls of Jericho 7 times and then shout. Let's use this example for a moment, but really understand the situation here. Jericho was a huge city, with the high walls that were seemingly impenetrable. So, the entire concept of simply marching around it 7 times and shouting seems quite impossible. Sounds like the realm of Faith. Now imagine being someone in the crowd marching for a moment. First, one time around the city is quite a walk, the city wasn't small.

Secondly, we've all just started marching together and our motivation is still high, and our Faith is still quite intact. Now, marching around a second and third lap, things are starting to get a little stale. We're almost halfway through and nothing has happened yet. The wall isn't crumbling, the people aren't running or screaming, the city isn't confused or fighting against each other, there are no signs of success or progress. Now let's fast forward to halfway through lap six, still nothing happening and no evidence that anything is working. Where's my Faith level now? Is the crowd around me beginning to doubt yet? Are there any silent and murmuring thoughts that fight against Faith? I'm willing to believe that if there were a moment for our adversary, Doubt, to step in, he's certainly got a foot in the door already about now.

In the example of Jericho, the Faith it took to walk lap one is the same Faith it takes to walk lap six, even after you don't see anything shifting, changing, or moving in your situation. The only thing that changes is doubt. The same Faith it takes to start, is the same Faith it takes to continue and to finish.

BEFORE YOU BEGIN, YOU MUST BE SET IN YOUR FAITH ENOUGH TO CONTINUE IN THE PRESENCE OF DOUBT. #FaithInitiated

Doubt comes from your mind, others' minds, and sometimes past experiences. Doubt's presence is toxic to any thought in your mind or goal and belief in your heart. Doubt doesn't attack our thoughts, our reality, or our Faith; it attacks our hope. If our hope is unstable, then sight becomes our crutch and primary source, and that is the opposing force to Faith. There is nothing anyone can accomplish when doubt is permitted to influence any part of our life. Doubt leads to a lack of hope, belief, vision, creativity, and a lack of confidence. Doubt can steer your Faith from a positive hope in the future to a closed-hand life stuck in accepting the world as it is. Routine and religion without evidence of progress can create doubt and allow comfort. Neither are helpful in the Kingdom of God, where Faith is mandatory. If you allow yourself to doubt, then the world will take every opportunity to supply for you only what it's willing to give, and you'll accept it every time.

I'VE ALWAYS BEEN ONE THAT'S BIG ON APPLICATION. AFTER ALL, WHAT GOOD IS INFORMATION IF IT CHANGES NOTHING?

#FaithInitiated If life started with knowing nothing at all, then learning would only happen through experience; the whole "the stove is hot, don't touch that" lesson. Our very nature of learning by experience and trying to verbally, or physically, explain it to someone else before they experience it, truly defines the importance of application to us as a human race. We wouldn't survive if it wasn't for application. Picture for a moment, your friend walks off a cliff, you watch him tumble down the cliff and die, then you follow them off the cliff, completely disregarding any information you just learned about walking off the cliff. We need others to teach us, we need everyone to be different and disagree, and we need people to experience different things and walks of life. More than that, we need those people to teach us about it and give us feedback or information about it, and to explain it clearly for us to receive the "how to" or "how not to" in the message and receive application.

Application is the path forward along which your Faith takes you. For example, when someone says, "that water is cold", it comes across as a fact we cannot change or affect, but we can't help but challenge the situation with questions or comments. However, when they say, "that frozen lake isn't solid, because my foot slipped in when the ice broke underneath me and I could have gotten hypothermia had I fallen in, but only my foot got wet, so I wouldn't go near it if I were you because my foot is still freezing cold." Now we understand the what, the how, and the why, which changes our perspective about the iced over lake. <u>APPLICATION MULTIPLIES THE CHANCES OF SUCCESS WITH EVERY NEW PIECE OF KNOWLEDGE AND INFORMATION PROVIDED. #FaithInitiated</u> That's why every greedy, selfish successful person doesn't want to give away the keys to success that they've discovered. In comparison, a Faith-centered leader sets an example, shares credit, brings others up with them, and breaks the barriers set by selfishness, hatred, envy, jealousy, and cynicism. The Faith-filled leader realizes that fulfilment isn't a competition and treasures the truly rare gems of hope, love, and Faith.

  The key to application is breaking down the information to find out what that information means to you, or what it should change in your situation. Learning is defined as: a change in behavior based on experience. However, a testimony is that experience I've had but broken down for you. When you hear of pain in someone's life that was caused by a certain thing, you attempt to stay away from it. Vise-Versa is when it comes to success, we try to mimic that thing or circumstance from their life into ours. With that said, have you ever tried to follow someone else's steps that succeeded in an area and found quickly that their methods didn't work for you? It doesn't mean their system is broken, but rather you needed to find that application of the knowledge of their success and customize it into your life. The overlooked step here is often figuring out who we are in truth, not in our perfect projected self image.

    Some have said that the definition of insanity is to keep doing the same thing but expecting a different result, but that's exactly what happens when we receive or hear information, testimony, experiences, and revelation but we don't change the way we do things by integrating that new knowledge into our lives, thus, leaving without application. That means you have the ability and knowledge to change your path to a better direction but refuse to expend energy to do it. Pastors across the world with healing ministries have used phrases like, "don't leave the hospital still sick with the doctor there in the room waiting for you", using the hospital as a metaphor for the church. Yet, every Sunday people see others healed and touched by God, they hear testimonies about it, they learn it from scriptures, and they still walk out sick without ever going forward for prayer. Why? No application, it doesn't make enough sense to them, they don't understand it, they don't believe it. It boils down to their Faith never being initiated. Their Faith sits dormant, holding the key to fulfilment and success in their very hand. They will never have real Faith if they merely discuss it from a place of comfort and without risk. Take risk, initiate Faith with action, and align your heart, mind, and mouth.

Now the question lies here, what will you do now? Faith is a multifaceted spiritual law that applies in many different situations and isn't confined by anything. By simply believing something so much that it necessitates new action in your life, you can change your environment, relationships, employers, family, finances, marriage, leadership, influence, mind, body, and most important your spirit. My prayer for you is that after reading this book you have picked up some knowledge that will allow you to be completely unlocked and free in your life. That you acknowledge who you are, pursuing your passions and desires, and change the world one day at a time. Start practicing having Faith in every situation for your sake and for others that are waiting for what you have inside. Exercise total freedom daily and remember to live your life for God and for yourself, not for others' expectations and opinions. Be free with full Faith.

Keep an eye out for book 2 of the Faith Initiated Series which brings more simple principles that will unlock your inner passions and desires. After unlocking your passion, the principles will easily flow which will propel your Faith walk and multiply your efforts.

NOTES

_____

_____

_____

_____

_____

_____

_____

_____

_____

_____

_____

FAITH APPENDIX

The following are some definitions of Faith beginning with Bible scripture definitions, then the Quran, Merriam-Webster, and personal definitions from a few books and some spiritual giants with their interpretation of Faith. Because there is more contained speaking about Faith in the rest of the book, I will not leave interpretations or comments after the scriptures in this section. I pray that God's Spirit shows you exactly what you need through the reading and studying of God's Word as He has done for me. I recommend you continue to re-read this section multiple times because each time is a new moment before God and will give you something different than before. Also, Faith comes by hearing, so read these definitions aloud, and as a good friend of mine used to always say, "watch and see". I will begin each Bible definition with the King James Version (KJV) and then use the New Living Translation (NLT) and the Message Translation (MSG) to compare and expound on some meanings.

Holy Bible:

Hebrews 11:1-3 –

- (KJV) Now Faith is the substance of things hoped for, the evidence of things not seen. ^{2} For by it the elders obtained a good report. ^{3} Through Faith we understand that the worlds were framed by the word of God, so that things which are seen were not made of things which do appear.
- (NLT) Faith shows the reality of what we hope for; it is the evidence of things we cannot see. ^{2} Through their Faith, the people in days of old earned a good reputation. ^{3} By Faith we understand that the entire universe was formed

at God's command, that what we now see did not come from anything that can be seen.

The word Faith used here in Hebrews 11:1-3 is the Greek word: **Pistis (G4102)** from the greek word Peitho (G3982) meaning to convince by argument true or false; to rely (by inward certainty); Usage: persuade (22 times), Trust (8 times), Obey (7 times), Have confidence (6 times), Believe (3 times), Be confident (2 times), Misc (7 times).

- **Definition**: Persuasion that is credence; moral conviction (of religious truth or the truthfulness of God or a religious teacher) especially reliance upon Christ for salvation.

- Occurs 228 times in the Bible with 239 references as Faith, 1 as assurance, 1 as belief, 1 as fidelity, 1 as them that believe, 1 as believe (with G1537 a primary preposition denoting origin is or point whence motion or action proceeds from)

Quran:

"Faith" (al-iman) in the Arabic language means to affirm something and to comply with it.

Ibn Taymiyyah writes:

It is understood that Faith is affirmation and not merely belief. Affirmation includes the words of the heart, which is belief, and the actions of the heart, which is compliance. Source: Majmu' Al-Fatawa 7/638

Hence, Faith in Islam means to believe in Allah, to affirm His truth, and to submit to His commands. The six pillars of Faith are to believe and affirm the following:

Allah, His angels, His messengers, His books, The Day of Judgment, Providence.

(https://abuaminaelias.com/the-definition-of-faith-in-islam/)

Dictionary.com:

- 1. Confidence or trust in a person or thing: *faith in another's ability.*

- 2. Belief that is not based on proof: *He had faith that the hypothesis would be substantiated by fact.*

- 3. Belief in God or in the doctrines or teachings of religion: *the firm faith of the Pilgrims.*

- 4. Belief in anything, as a code of ethics, standards of merit, etc.: *to be of the same faith with someone concerning honesty.*

- 5. A system of religious belief: *the Christian faith; the Jewish faith.*

- 6. The obligation of loyalty or fidelity to a person, promise, engagement, etc.: *Failure to appear would be breaking faith.*

- 7. The observance of this obligation; fidelity to one's promise, oath, allegiance, etc.:

  He was the only one who proved his faith during our recent troubles.

- 8. *Christian Theology;* the trust in God and in His promises as made

  through Christ and the Scriptures by which humans are justified or saved.

Merriam Webster:

- *a* : Allegiance to duty or a person : loyalty lost *faith* in the company's president*b (1)* : fidelity to one's promises *(2)* : sincerity of intentions acted in good *faith*

- *a (1)* : Belief and trust in and loyalty to God *(2)* : belief in the traditional doctrines of a religion*b (1)* : firm belief in something for which there is no proof clinging to the *faith* that her missing son would one day return *(2)* : complete trust.

- Something that is believed especially with strong conviction; *especially* : a system of religious beliefs the Protestant *faith*

Think and Grow Rich:

The following quotes are different definitions of Faith from the book Think and Grow Rich by Napoleon Hill.

- "Faith is the head chemist of the mind."
- "Faith is a state of mind which may be induced, or created, by affirmation or repeated instructions to the subconscious mind, through the principle of autosuggestion."
- "Faith is the "eternal elixir" which gives life, power, and action to the impulse of thought."
- "Faith is the starting point of all accumulation of riches."

- "Faith is the basis of all miracles, and all mysteries which cannot be analyzed by the rules of science."
- "Faith is the only known antidote for failure."
- "Faith is the element, the "chemical" which, when mixed with prayer, gives one direct communication with Infinite Intelligence."
- "Faith is the element which transforms the ordinary vibration of thought, created by the finite mind of man, into the spiritual equivalent."
- "Faith is the only agency through which the cosmic force of Infinite Intelligence can be harnessed and used by man."

Personal Quotes:

"Faith is the willingness to give truly and wholly of one's self to an idea or set of ideas which defines one's own personal beliefs." - Will Wilson

"Faith from my experience is having the utmost confidence in something you strongly believe, and no matter what anyone says, not the circumstances, you cannot be shaken, mislead, or detoured from your belief." - DeQuaan Simmons

"Our Faith is the application of our prayers being answered." - DaAshlynn Duis

"Faith: Mountain mover." – Jimmy Davidson Jr.

"Faith: the pillar on which prayers are answered."
- Christie Faye

"Faith is believing in yourself and those around you to accomplish anything. Waking up on the daily and saying, "I believe I can accomplish this" or, "I believe you can accomplish this". I've experienced it first-hand." – Jack Kypreos

"Faith is, 'I don't care what the reality is, God can accomplish anything'. Faith is knowing even in the middle of the day-to-day storms of life we will get through everything, despite what it looks like. We have Faith already in so many things, like flipping a switch expecting lights to come on before there's any evidence that they will." – Bret Stone

"Faith; the proof of what is not yet seen or experienced, which we use as confidence in its existence. It's why we prepare for and go after something, even though we haven't seen or experienced it yet." – Kristopher Jones

"Faith is knowing that you were preordained before the foundation of the earth that you are called to be in subjection to God's word, and that He will prepare you for the work that needs to be done."

– Carolyn Scott

"Faith is knowing what you've been entrusted with and what you're capable of, but knowing you are so small and yet so important to the Father. Faith is what connects us to what we are and what we could become. Faith is knowing and believing that you are created to do great things, it is also knowing that you were created to serve. Without Faith we are lost and disconnected from what creates us and what drives us to purpose and meaning."

– Aaron Jacobs

"Faith is the forward movement in our life derived from a set belief in our future, so solidly convinced, that it's results not happening is no longer a reality."

– Stephen Stone

"Faith is a concept that employs the force of multiplication to increase the focus of your Faith."

– Stephen Stone

Made in the USA
Middletown, DE
10 February 2021